GETTING TO KNOW THE WORLD'S GREATEST ARTISTS

VAN GOGH

WRITTEN AND ILLUSTRATED BY MIKE VENEZIA

CHILDRENS PRESS ®

CHICAGO

Dedicated to George and Anne
A special thanks to Sarah Mollman

Cover: *Olive Trees*. 1889. Oil on canvas.
The Minneapolis Institute of Arts

Library of Congress Cataloging-in-Publication Data

Venezia, Mike.
    Van Gogh / by Mike Venezia.
        p.   cm. — (Getting to know the world's greatest
artists)
    Summary: Briefly examines the life and work of the
nineteenth-century Dutchman who was one of the greatest
artists of all time.
    ISBN 0-516-02274-1
    1.   Gogh, Vincent van, 1853-1890—Criticism and
interpretation—Juvenile literature.   [1.   Gogh, Vincent
van, 1853-1890.   2.   Artists.   3.   Painting,
Dutch.   4.   painting, Modern-Netherlands.   5.   Art
appreciation.]   I.   Title.   II.   Series.
ND653.G7V46   1988   88-11842
759.9492—dc19   CIP
[92]   AC

Childrens Press®, Chicago
Copyright ©1988 by Regensteiner Publishing Enterprises, Inc.
All rights reserved. Published simultaneously in Canada.
Printed in the United States of America.
        7 8 9 10 R 97 96

Self Portrait. 1886-1887. Panel, 41.0 x 32.5 cm. © 1988 The Art Institute of Chicago

Vincent van Gogh was one of the most tragic artists who ever lived.

Nothing ever seemed to go right for him and he wasn't very happy.

He never even smiled in his self-portraits.

Van Gogh was born in Holland in 1853 and died in France in 1890. Unlike most artists, van Gogh didn't decide to become a painter until he was grown up.

He tried a lot of other things first.

He worked in an art gallery selling paintings. He tried teaching. He worked in a bookstore and he was a preacher like his dad.

None of these things made him very happy. Then one day he decided to be an artist.

(top left) *Miners*. 1880. Pencil, 17½ x 22 cm.
State Museum Kröller-Müller,
Otterlo, the Netherlands

(top right) *Peasant Walking with Stick*.
1885. Black chalk, 13½ x 7½ cm.
State Museum Kröller-Müller,
Otterlo, the Netherlands

(bottom) *Sand Pit with Men at Work*. 1883.
Pencil. Vincent Van Gogh Foundation/
National Museum Vincent Van Gogh,
Amsterdam

Van Gogh always tried his best at whatever he did, so he went to different art schools to learn everything he could about drawing and painting. His early drawings were of the poor people he used to help when he was a preacher.

Sien with Child on Lap. 1883. Black chalk, 16¼ x 17¼ cm.
State Museum Kröller-Müller, Otterlo, the Netherlands

On the Road. 1881. Black chalk. Vincent Van Gogh Foundation/
National Museum Vincent Van Gogh, Amsterdam

There are certain things you can
see in these drawings that show up
later in his famous paintings, such as
the strong lines and shapes. You can
see the feelings he had for everyday
people.

Potato Eaters, Nuenun. 1885. Oil on canvas.
Vincent Van Gogh, Foundation/National Museum Vincent Van Gogh, Amsterdam

Van Gogh's first paintings were also of the poor people he had been helping. In this painting, the family was so poor they had only a few potatoes to eat for dinner. They look tired and not very happy.

Two Women in the Peat. 1883. Oil on canvas.
Vincent Van Gogh Foundation/National Museum Vincent Van Gogh, Amsterdam

The colors in van Gogh's early paintings are dark and sad.

He wanted everyone to know how hard the lives of the poor people were.

Van Gogh kept using dark colors
until he discovered some very
colorful Japanese artwork. He loved
the bright colors and strong lines and
shapes that he saw.

Farmhouse in Provence, Arles. 1888. Oil on canvas. National Gallery of Art, Washington, D.C.

Soon van Gogh's paintings started to look much more colorful.

Look at the difference between the gloomy *Potato Eaters* and the painting above, which was done only a few years later.

We know a lot about how van Gogh felt, and why he did certain things, because he was always writing letters to his younger brother, Theo.

Theo always helped his brother. He encouraged him to paint and sent him money when he could.

The Postman Roulin, Arles. 1889. Oil on canvas.
State Museum Kröller-Müller, Otterlo, the Netherlands

Because van Gogh was always sending and receiving letters, he got to know his postman pretty well. He painted pictures of him and used the postman's wife as a model in many of his paintings as well.

In 1886 Vincent moved to Paris, France, to join Theo.

Paris was the center of the art world then. Since Theo was in the business of buying and selling paintings, and Vincent wanted to be an artist, it seemed like a pretty good place to be.

Theo introduced Vincent to a lot of painters while they lived in Paris.

Hardly anyone knew it then, but many of those painters would become world-famous artists someday.

A couple of years later, Vincent van Gogh decided to leave Paris and move to a small country town called Arles.

Van Gogh thought Arles would be a great place for artists to get together to paint and talk about their different ideas. He tried very hard to get as many artists as he could to join him. The only one to try it out was Paul Gauguin, although he wasn't really crazy about the idea.

It turned out to be a big mistake.

Gauguin didn't seem to like
anything van Gogh did in Arles.
They argued a lot.

Van Gogh probably decided to listen to Gauguin about cleaning the place up, because his bedroom looks pretty neat in this painting.

Bedroom at Arles. 1888. Oil on canvas, 73.6 x 92.3 cm. © 1988 The Art Institute of Chicago

Finally, after a very bad argument, Gauguin decided to leave van Gogh and return to Paris.

Van Gogh didn't know what to do. He really wanted things to work out well with Gauguin.

Van Gogh had always had problems during his life with the way he felt. Sometimes he would get so angry and upset that no one could make him feel better. This time he became so angry and upset he cut off part of his ear!

Self-Portrait with Bandaged Ear. 1889. Oil on canvas. Courtauld Institute Galleries, London

Van Gogh painted pictures of himself after this happened.

It looks like he wished he hadn't done it.

Vincent van Gogh never really got better after Gauguin left him.

The Starry Night. 1889. Oil on Canvas, 73.7 x 92.1 cm. The Museum of Modern Art, New York

Sometimes he was too angry to paint, and sometimes he was too sad to paint. When he felt good, he painted better than ever.

He made the stars in *The Starry Night* seem like they're really shining.

Cypresses. 1889. Oil on canvas, 93.3 x 74 cm. The Metropolitan Museum of Art, New York

The trees in this painting look like flames, and it feels like the whole picture is moving.

In this painting
van Gogh made the
sun look really hot.
You almost feel
like you should put
sunglasses on to
look at it.

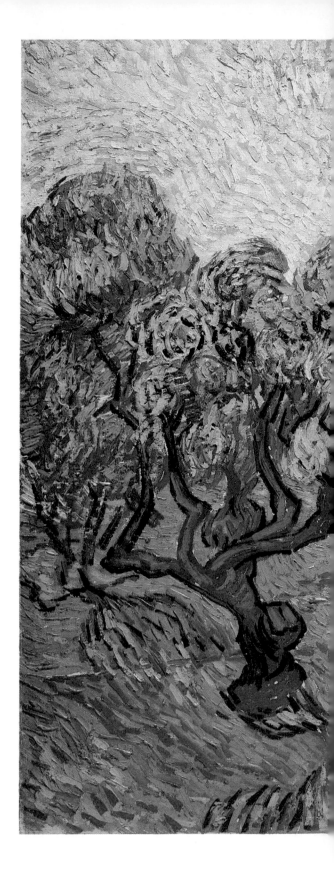

Olive Trees. 1889. Oil on canvas. The Minneapolis Institute of Arts

Detail, *Sunflowers*. 1888. Oil on canvas. Scala/ Art Resource

Van Gogh usually put his paint on very thick. Sometimes he painted so fast he didn't even mix his colors. He used paint right out of the tube.

Van Gogh used so much paint he was always running out. Sometimes he stopped buying food in order to buy more paint, so he was hungry a lot of the time, and he wasn't healthy.

Hardly anyone was interested in van Gogh's work while he was alive. He sold only a few drawings and maybe one or two paintings. People in the 1880s and 1890s just weren't used to the bright "moving" pictures that van Gogh made.

Today things are different. People have learned how beautiful Vincent van Gogh's art is.

Now his paintings are some of the most popular in the world.

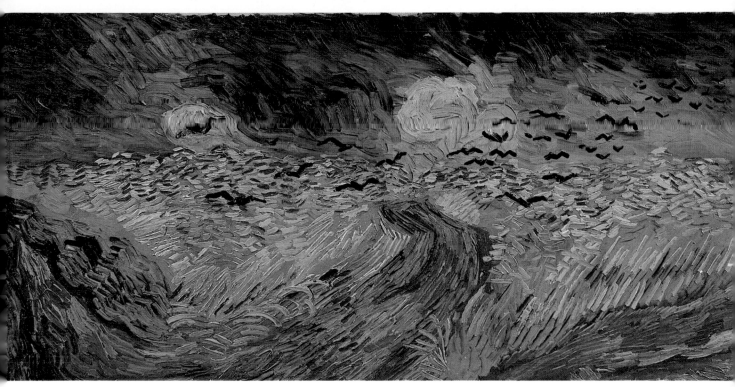

Wheatfield with Crows. 1890. Oil on canvas.
Vincent Van Gogh Foundation/National Museum Vincent Van Gogh, Amsterdam

This may have been van Gogh's last painting. Some people think it shows how angry and upset he must have been feeling because he painted a scary sky, roads that led to a dark background, and crows that look like bats.

Soon after this painting was finished, van Gogh shot himself. He died two days later.

Van Gogh made
his paintings seem
alive with color.
   His colors are
so bright and
beautiful you can
almost smell
the flowers he
painted, or feel
the bright sun.

Sunflowers. 1888. Oil on canvas. Scala/Art Resource

*Garden of
the Poets.*
1888.
Oil on canvas,
73 x 92.1 cm.
© 1988, The Art
Institute
of Chicago

30

His brush strokes give everything a feeling of movement. Trees, stars, and people feel alive.

L'Arlesienne. 1888. Oil on canvas. 91.4 x 73.7 cm.
The Metropolitan Museum of Art, New York

The Night Cafe, 1888. Oil on canvas.
Yale University Art Gallery at the Bequest
of Stephen Carlton Clark, B.A. 1903

Olive Grove. 1889. Oil on canvas.
State Museum Kröller-Müller, Otterlo, the Netherlands

Maybe more than any other artist, van Gogh's feelings came out in his paintings. That's why Vincent van Gogh is one of the world's greatest artists.

It's much better to see a real Vincent van Gogh painting than a picture of one. It's fun to see how thick he put his paint on, his brush strokes, and how bright his colors are.

The pictures in this book came from the museums listed below. If none of them is close to you, maybe you can visit one when you are on vacation.

The Art Institute of Chicago
Courtauld Institute Galleries, London
The Metropolitan Museum of Art, New York
The Minneapolis Institute of Arts
The Museum of Modern Art, New York
National Gallery of Art, Washington, D.C.
State Museum Kröller-Müller, Otterlo, the Netherlands
Vincent Van Gogh Foundation / National Museum Vincent Van Gogh, Amsterdam
Yale University Art Gallery, New Haven, Connecticut